The Word Has Come Down

Six Midweek Monologues and Services for Lent

Beth Huener

CSS Publishing Co.
Lima, Ohio

THE WORD HAS COME DOWN

FIRST EDITION
Copyright © 2011
by CSS Publishing Co.

Published by CSS Publishing Company, Inc., Lima, Ohio 45807. All rights reserved. No part of this publication may be reproduced in any manner whatsoever without the prior permission of the publisher, except in the case of brief quotations embodied in critical articles and reviews. Inquiries should be addressed to: CSS Publishing Company, Inc., Permissions Department, 5450 N. Dixie Highway, Lima, Ohio 45807.

Scripture quotations marked (NRSV) are from the New Revised Standard Version of the Bible, copyright 1989 by the Division of Christian Education of the National Council of the Churches of Christ in the USA. Used by permission.

Library of Congress Cataloging-in-Publication Data
Huener, Beth.
   The Word has come down : six midweek Monologues and Services for Lent / Beth Huener. -- 1st Ed.
     p. cm.
   Summary: "Six midweek Lenten services including Ash Wednesday, Maundy Thursday, Good Friday, and Easter Sunrise"--Provided by publisher.
     ISBN 0-7880-2635-6 (alk. paper)
   1. Lent. 2. Worship programs. I. Title. II. Title: Six midweek Monologues and Services for Lent.

BV85.H765 2011
263'.92--dc22
                                                2010052176

ISBN-13: 978-0-7880-2635-5
ISBN-10: 0-7880-2635-6   PRINTED IN USA

*These services are dedicated
to the Christians gathering at
First St. Mark's Lutheran Church in Oregon, Ohio,
on whose behalf they were created.*

Table of Contents

Ash Wednesday Worship Service	7
The First Midweek Service The Witness of Judas, Disciple and Betrayer of Jesus	15
The Second Midweek Service The Witness of Peter	23
The Third Midweek Service The Witness of Caiaphas, High Priest	31
The Fourth Midweek Service The Witness of Herod, Tetrarch of Jerusalem	39
The Fifth Midweek Service The Witness of Pontius Pilate, Roman Governor of Israel	47
Maundy Thursday Service	55
Good Friday The Witness of the Crowd	63
Easter Sunrise Service	71

ASH WEDNESDAY WORSHIP SERVICE

Opening Hymn
"Chief of Sinners Though I Be"

First Lesson
Joel 2:12-19

Second Lesson
2 Corinthians 5:21b—6:2
The Imposition of Ashes
(Upon the imposition of the ashes, the pastor will say: "Remember that you are dust and to dust you shall return. Repent and believe in the gospel.")

Gospel
Matthew 6:1-6, 16-21

Homily
Remember that you are dust and to dust you shall return. Why has the church set this day apart for us? There does not seem to be anything in the Bible about it. And truth to tell, understanding that our Lord's gospel is joyous news, could this observance that should be called at least somber, be considered heretical as anything that contradicts the gospel must be? Besides, in our world, we never cease to be inundated with images of death; why do we need to be reminded that we will die? It could be that this day the church has set apart and observed for over 1,000 years is not intended to remind us that we will die.

Ash Wednesday is not like one of those T-shirts you might see every now and again: T-shirts that say things like "Don't wait until 11:45 for the midnight hour! It might come at 11:30!" It is not like a tract you receive in the mall, which says underneath a cartoon of a man sweating in a room enclosed with fire: "You think you are hot now, wait till you live the in the fast lane for eternity!"

Ash Wednesday is like the entire gospel story. It is an invitation. It is not a warning. The Bible does not have to issue warnings. An honest look at the world and even at our own lives is all the warning we need. These T-shirts and tracts and many of the sermons that have been preached over the 2,000 years have simply told us what we already know. We are in trouble. Ash Wednesday says, "Yes, you are, but you began with God and it is with God you may end." God created us out of the ground and to the ground we will return. But that does not mean that God has let us go. It might be helpful for us to understand where the whole idea of Ash Wednesday came from.

At one point in my life, I believed that it came from the Jewish custom of sitting in ashes, as though you were thrown out with the ashes. To sit in the ashes is to sit in the garbage. This is how I show the world how I feel, whether it is because I am ashamed or I am sad, life as it was yesterday is no longer possible. But this interpretation makes no sense.

A look at our gospel the church has appointed for us centuries ago tells us that we are to put aside all outward demonstrations of sorrow and to approach God and the world with courage and humility. So where did this observance come from? It came from France before it was France when it was still Gaul, filled with wild and pagan tribesmen who lived far away from the great cities of the south and far away from any cathedral or even any building that could be called a church. Still, even 1,500 years ago, there were already Christians in that far away place — faithful priests who brought the message of salvation.

Somehow, the people who heard these words from the book of Genesis in which God warns man: Remember you are dust and to dust you shall return, saw an invitation to believe in the gospel — not a warning. Far away and long ago, Christian people were less concerned about saying the right thing and more concerned about remembering what was true. To remember God's presence in their lives, they took something that all people always had. Ashes. We are just like this. And because of God's forgiveness, even though we are just like this, just like dust and ashes we have been redeemed.

Perhaps we are confused about Ash Wednesday because, unlike most people who have ever lived on this planet, ashes are not an ordinary thing in most of our lives. But ashes are what was left after people throughout most of history finished firing a kiln to make utensils, heating a pot to cook soup, building a fire to keep warm, or setting up a sentry post to keep safe.

Now most pastors have to go out and find ashes. Over the last 100 years it has become traditional to burn dried palm fronds from the previous Palm Sunday. I have never gotten that to work. Besides, I don't think that that is what this observance is all about. It is not that we have been anointed with this special thing we have saved in a dry place for almost a year. It is that we have been redeemed by God so that we may build fires in the world to fire a kiln to make utensils, heat a pot to cook soup, build a fire to keep warm, or set up a sentry post to keep safe. We have been redeemed to feed and clothe, to equip and protect.

Out of this ordinariness, out of that which is the most common human experience, death, God gives us the power to feed and clothe, to equip and protect. It is not a warning. It is an invitation to listen to the gospel and share our gift of salvation.

A Primitive Hymn by Isaac Watts sung to "St. Anne" the tune of "O God Our Help in Ages Past"

> Why do we mourn departing friends
> Or shake at death's alarms?
> 'Tis but the voice that Jesus sends
> To call them to His arms.
>
> Why should we tremble to convey
> Their bodies to the tomb?
> There the dear flesh of Jesus lay,
> And left a long perfume.
>
> Thence he arose, ascending high,
> And showed our feet the way.
> Up to the Lord our flesh shall fly
> At the great rising day.

The Offering

Psalm 51

The Confession of Sins
Pastor: Today, as we begin Lent's dark journey, the days lengthen as we look deeply into ourselves and in our deepest needs. As the days grow warmer, we are held in God's loving embrace as we face the reality of our sinful states. As we do this, we are upheld by God's word of promise as we say the words that reveal our failing and declare our faith. Let us pray.
Left Side: When we fail to bring your love into consideration or when we slip into apathy or despair about the world.
Right side: When we fail to take strength and courage from the example of your Son.

Left Side: When by our inaction, we allow injustice, greed, selfishness, and even cruelty to go unchecked.

Right side: When by our inaction, we allow your truth to go unspoken and undefended, ignored and mocked.

All: Though we are unworthy, Lord, forgive us.

Left Side: When with our apathy and despair, we fall into dangerous, abusive, and destructive habits,

Right side: or allow our hopelessness to turn into cynicism or the deadly desire for power, wealth, or other forms of earthly corruptible security.

All: Though we are unworthy, Lord, forgive us.

Left Side: When in our weakness and fear, we allow ourselves to be dragged down into a place where we see no way to live that does not involve sinful behavior,

Right side: and perhaps find our strength and our courage in sin instead of in your goodness.

All: Though we are unworthy, Lord, forgive us.

Left Side: When we find profane power and treacherous security in acts of injustice, greed, selfishness, and cruelty.

Right side: And allow others to pay the cost for that power and security

All: Though we are unworthy, Lord, forgive us.

Left Side: When we neglect the truth your Son died to show us, when we abuse those who try to spread that truth with words and actions with our fearful doubt and our lack of support.

Right side: When we show the world how little your love really means to us.

All: Though we are unworthy, Lord, forgive us.

Pastor: We stand before you, dear Lord, knowing you have already forgiven us. Help us to listen as you speak your word of acceptance, your word of mercy, and your word of redemption.

All: In the name of your Son we pray. Amen.

Holy Communion
The Word of Institution for Ash Wednesday
Pastor: Great God in heaven, you sent your Son to take on our condition and, being sinless, to die for our sin. Raising him from death, you sent your Spirit to help us understand things that are too beautiful for us to see. We give thanks for these beautiful and incomprehensible things that conquer our fear and free us for service. Break us from our chains, Lord, and bind us to your will, which your Son so humbly obeyed.
Congregation: At his invitation, we pray. Amen.

The Words of Institution

The Lord's Prayer
Post Communion Prayer
Pastor: We give you thanks, Lord, that you have welcomed us, unworthy as we are, into your presence. Fill us with a gratitude born of the knowledge of your Son's sacrifice and send us forth to come to understand the freedom and joy this sacrifice can mean.
Congregation: Amen.

The Closing Prayer
Pastor: Accomplish in us, O God, the work of your salvation,
Congregation: that we may show forth your glory in the world.
Pastor: By the cross and the Passion of your Son, our Lord,
Congregation: bring us with all your saints to the joy of his resurrection.
Pastor: Almighty God, the Father of our Lord Jesus Christ, does not desire the death of sinners; rather that we may turn from our wickedness and live. Therefore, we implore him to grant us true repentance and his Holy Spirit that those things

we do this day, may please him, that the rest of our lives may be pure and holy, and that at the last we may come to his eternal joy, through Jesus Christ, our Lord.
Congregation: Amen.

Hymn
"Beneath the Cross of Jesus"

The congregation will leave in silence.

THE FIRST MIDWEEK SERVICE

The Witness of Judas
Disciple and Betrayer of Jesus

The Story of Judas
Matthew 26:14-15, 21-26, 45-50; 27:3-5

Opening Hymn
"Alas! And Did My Savior Bleed"

The Witness: Judas
I am Judas, one of the disciples of Jesus. I will tell you how I came to know Jesus in a minute. First, I want to object to what the stories about Jesus you call the gospels say about me. I am not the evil man these stories say I am. It is true that I did betray Jesus, but as you will see, I had reasons to do so.

I was one of his disciples; the only one from Judea. The rest were Galileans. Most were related to each other. I was an outsider from the start. Only Matthew, the tax collector, and I had some schooling. I was our treasurer. Jesus trusted me with what little money there was.

The way Jesus called us was strange. He just said to follow him. No details about where or why. Just follow him. But there was something about him that made me go with him.

He was a holy man, dedicated to God. And I loved him as much as the others did.

At first, we were waiting for the Messiah sent from God. We were sure Jesus was him. Instead of helping us get rid of the Romans, he told us we should love them and pray for them.

The people who followed him were tax collectors, prostitutes, and beggars, and he welcomed them. Then there

15

was the law of Moses. He broke it! He said the law was made for humanity — not that humanity was made for the law. As if God's law is not as important as the people he ate and drank with.

At that point, I don't know whether I believed he was the Messiah or not.

The temple priests wanted to get Jesus for a long time. They were afraid of him. They were afraid he would lead the people against them. And they were afraid to take him on their own. They needed me. And they paid me to help them.

I didn't do it for the money.

They wanted to get him at night without a lot of people around.

Yes. They didn't want any trouble. They needed my help. We found him in the garden that overlooks the city. He was with some of his followers.

The chief priest was afraid of trouble. He sent armed police with me to make the arrest. Jesus didn't resist, but Peter went wild. Then Jesus stopped the trouble and went quietly. The others there — they all ran — afraid of being arrested too.

They convicted and executed him. He claimed to be the Messiah, but he didn't help overthrow the Romans. He didn't follow the laws of Moses. He ate and drank with all kinds of sinners. If he was the Messiah, Jesus sure had a strange way of showing it.

Opening Prayer
Pastor: Let us pray:
Congregation: Dear God in heaven, we lay before you our own authority, confusion, and remorse. We pray that your mercy covers all sins, even those as grave as Judas'. Forgive all who refuse the mercy your Son's death brought us. Fill us with such an awareness of your deep

love that despair has no place in our lives. In his name, we pray. Amen.

Authority

A Reading
1 Samuel 8:4-18

A Meditation
We are so hungry for someone to take charge of our lives. I know that's not how we usually think of ourselves. But we truly need someone to take charge of our lives, or at the very least find someone or something to rely on. I remember I read a few different novels in the early '80s and to tell you the truth, I don't even remember the names of these novels, but in each case, the main character was a bad guy. They both had similarities. In both cases, these men had been trained in some official capacity to be assassins, but their similarities went deeper than that. Physically, they were both beautiful and they both had iron wills, but they were also completely devoid of kindness. There was one other characteristic that they shared. They were both the product of not only completely different races, but also completely different cultures and each case they had embraced the culture of one parent and had abandoned the culture of the other. Once again, in both cases, this rejection of the authority of one parent had left them, not confused, but embittered to the point of steel.

As I said, I read two novels that told the story of this same beautiful kind of monster. But I don't recall having seen this kind of character emerge in the last twenty years or so. I think he is too horrible to contemplate. Authority is such an integral thing in our lives that it is painful to imagine having to embrace the authority of one parent only at the cost of rejecting the other parent's culture entirely. It is painful,

I think, because it is something that the mature person must do.

The word authority comes from the Latin word *auctoritas* that was used largely as a legal term meaning precedent. So being under another's authority is a great way to escape blame.

What does it mean for a young person to move out on their own? It means to accept authority over their own lives which they had previously assumed was their parents. What is marriage but the transfer or at least the sharing of authority over one's life with someone else? What does it mean to take a job? It means the same thing. It means that for so many hours a day we transfer the authority over our lives to someone else. While we do not become their slaves, we have agreed to do certain tasks during those hours.

But for the Christian, authority means that we obey God before our parents, our spouses, or our employers. That also means we trust God more as well. Authority is painful when our trust and obedience to God conflict with all the other forces that hold sway over our lives. Had poor Judas understood where true authority lay, he would not have allowed the authority of the Jews to confuse him.

Pastor: Let us pray:
Congregation: Direct us, O Lord, in all our doings with your most gracious favor and further us with your continual help that in all our works, begun, continued, and ended in you, we may glorify your holy name and finally, by your mercy, obtain everlasting life, through Jesus Christ, our Lord. Amen.

Primitive Hymn by Joseph Hart sung to "Rathbun" the tune of "In the Cross of Christ I Glory"

Come, ye sinners, poor and needy,
Weak and wounded, sick and sore;
Jesus ready stands to save you,
Full of pity, love, and power.

Come, ye thirsty, come, and welcome,
God's free bounty glorify;
True belief and true repentance,
Every grace that brings you nigh.

Come, ye weary, heavy laden,
Lost and ruined by the fall;
If you tarry till you're better,
You will never come at all.

View him prostrate in the garden;
On the ground your Maker lies.
On the bloody tree behold him;
Sinner, will this not suffice?

Lo! th'incarnate God ascended,
Pleads the merit of his blood:
Venture on him, venture wholly,
Let no other trust intrude.

Let not conscience make you linger,
Not of fitness fondly dream;
All the fitness he requireth
Is to feel your need of him.

Confusion

A Reading
Job 10:2-22

A Meditation

I remember an old sitcom about a young man who was on jury duty. He asked the judge if he could come and visit with him, and you can tell that it's a sitcom because the judge said yes. Only in television would a jurist show such largesse. Who knows, it might even be against the law. In any case, the judge was more than patient when the young man told him that he was confused by the differing testimony that he was hearing. In fact, he said he was glad to hear it. The judge told him that what he was experiencing was not confusion but sophisticated thinking. The world is a confusing place said the judge and only a child or a fool thinks otherwise. So it makes sense that the word confusion comes from the Latin *confundere* meaning to mix. So that leaves us with a question.

Does Christianity un-confuse them? Do the ethics of Christianity iron things out? And if so, if Judas was one of Jesus' followers, why was he so confused? Was it a problem with authority? Maybe. Perhaps he did not believe himself worthy of the love and forgiveness Jesus offered and wanted to take himself out of Jesus' sphere of influence before his unworthiness was discovered. Or maybe it could be something even more basic. Was it an inability to take in such good news? I have come to believe that incomprehensible blessing is a big reason why Christianity is often so confusing for people.

You will hear it said that people are always trying to get something for nothing. But deep down, they always know that someone somewhere will have to pay for what they get. Everyone, even a child knows that there is nothing for free.

Did Judas' actions result from the fear that eventually all of Jesus' warm talk about love and forgiveness was one day going to have to be paid for? Both of his suppositions were correct. He was not worthy and all of Jesus' love and forgiveness had to be paid for. Not because God demanded it, but because we are confused, eternally confused. We are unworthy and we know it. We do want forgiveness, but we are afraid, desperately afraid that we will, somehow, somewhere, have to pay for the mercy he has given us. The key is to understand that, though we are not worthy, though our lives must be marked with remorse, God's love has freed us from all the nails of our sin by showing us the nail prints in the hands of his Son.

Pastor: Let us pray:
Congregation: Dear God in heaven, comfort us with your presence made sweet in prayer, powerful in witness and purposeful in community. Forgive us when we allow our confusion or our despair to sink us into inaction or worse yet, betrayal. Open our hearts to your presence. In the name of your Son, we pray. Amen.

Remorse

A Reading
Psalm 38

A Meditation
With just a casual glance at the life of Judas, one might feel that remorse is exactly what he should have been feeling after he betrayed his Lord. But remorse is an ugly word; so I looked it up in the dictionary and it comes from the French words meaning to bite again. Remorse is to allow a regret to eat away at you. That is exactly what Judas allowed to happen to him. He did not accept the authority of God and the confusion that caused him to betray brought about the remorse that killed him.

Now, before we go any further, I want to say that anyone can get lost. The faster our world moves, the quicker people can lose their way. It only takes a moment, especially if there is a bridge, some pills, a gun, or as in Judas' case, a rope close at hand. I would advise us all, therefore, against doubting for one moment God's mercy in such a case.

Confusion and competing authorities hold sway in this earthbound plane and none of us are free from them. That is why we must not only accept that fact, but also be open to God's gifts. We must do what we have no choice to do and what Judas did not do. He did not ask forgiveness of his Lord. He did not seek out his family of faith. He gave in to despair. That is what he did do, but what he did not do was even more significant. He did not ask forgiveness of his Lord. He did not seek out his family of faith for support. We need to be that family of faith for each other because whether we admit it or not, we all betray our Savior every day.

Offering

The Prayers of the People

The Lord's Prayer

Closing Hymn
"O Sacred Head Now Wounded"

THE SECOND MIDWEEK SERVICE

The Witness of Peter
Matthew 14:22-30; 17:29-36; 26:67-75

Opening Hymn
"Christ the Life of All the Living"

Meditation
I had always been the one. At least I had always thought I was the one. I was the one who was always there for Jesus. I was always the one who knew just what to say. All the rest of them were either so negative or just silent that it killed me to have Jesus stand there feeling like none of us were getting it. Well, it turned out that none of us were getting it. Least of all, me. But I just couldn't hack the silence. So I filled it.

It turned out to be a bad habit. I should have remained silent that terrible night. I can't say I know what would have happened to me had I done so, but whatever it was, it would have been better than what did happen. Because of what I said, now I have a burden I will never ever shake. And the worst part about it is that he warned me that it would happen. And as usual, I didn't listen. Had I, I might have avoided feeling the way I am feeling. I have come to the conclusion that feeling, wanting to feel a certain way, wanting to keep feeling a certain way, not wanting to feel a certain way, one way or another, feeling has been the root of my problem all along. When Jesus took us up to that mountain, and we saw him looking almost like God, and we saw him there with who we knew had to be Moses and Elijah, I never wanted to stop feeling the way I was feeling, feeling like I was in the presence of God and his greatest servants.

Well, according to the two Zebedee kids, I sounded pretty stupid, like I wanted us all to stay up there and live there.

Well, I didn't care then what they thought, and I don't care now. I still wish we were up there. Things were a lot clearer up there. And that feeling stayed with me for a long time. But even before that, I knew. Earlier, Jesus asked us who we thought he was. As usual, I was the only one who spoke up. "You are the Christ of God," I told Jesus. I was so sure. All I ever wanted was to be with Jesus. Even when Jesus was walking on the water. If he could do it, I believed I could too as long as I stayed with Jesus. And he asked me. He asked me to come out with him. For a split second there, I felt safe. Then I felt the wind and I saw the wave and I didn't feel safe anymore. That's sort of how I felt on that night.

After we fell asleep there in Gethsemane, I told myself I wasn't going to let him down ever again. I tried. I really did. I was the only one who stayed. Well, it was me and the younger Zebedee kid, you know, the squirt, John. But you know, nobody pays attention to kids. Anyway, things were going all right until that one maid came up to me and asked me if I knew Jesus. Suddenly, all I felt was fear. Instead of feeling that Jesus loved me, I thought about how he couldn't help me now. He couldn't even help himself. So I denied ever even knowing him. Now, for the rest of my life, no matter what I feel, I will always feel ashamed.

Opening Prayer
Pastor: Let us pray:
Congregation: Great God in heaven, quell our fear, dispel our remorse, and humble us before your might, your forgiveness, and your love. Teach us that we need never live without any of them. In the name of your Son, we pray. Amen.

Fear

A Reading
Numbers 14:1-4

The word fear comes from an old English word that means not fear but something of which we are often afraid. It comes from the word for ambush. I found that very instructive considering the fact that whenever I think of Peter's fear, I think most powerfully of the moment when he saw the wave coming at him, as he saw the wind ambush him. For years, I thought I had misinterpreted what happened on that day when Peter asked our Lord if he could come out onto the water and join him.

When I was younger, I thought that the error Peter made was in losing faith when he saw the wave. Later in my life, I came to the conclusion that he made the error long before then. I believe his error was in thinking he had to try to show Jesus what he was made of. Before we go ahead with this theme, I have to tell you that this story, like many in the gospel, brings up a lot of questions for me.

First of all, why was Jesus on the water in the first place? The only rational explanation would be that he wished to communicate his power to his disciples. Were that the case, then truly, Jesus should have expected one of the boys, probably Peter, to try to join him on the waves. For years, I thought that the sin Peter committed was in thinking he had to show Jesus what he was made of. I no longer believe that to be a sin.

It is true that Peter gave into his fear. But what he did with his fear was exactly what he was supposed to do. It is true that in denying his Lord, Peter showed his fear. Only instead of clinging to his Savior in that courtyard outside the high priest's palace, he denied him. Peter made the right choice out there on the waves. In what was probably his attempt to show Jesus what he was made of, or just as probably in his desire to, no matter what, be where his Savior was, Peter found himself in trouble out there on the waves. But he made a good choice. True, fear out there on the Sea of Galilee was his problem, but by reaching out for his Savior, he reached out for salvation. Outside the high priest's palace, he took the same option the children of Israel facing the armies of Canaan. He chose to retrench, to back up into the trap of the known, the despair of the familiar, and let his Savior die alone.

Pastor: Let us pray:
Congregation: Protect us from the danger of getting in our own way and blocking our experience of you. Our pride, along with our fear, can lure us away from the only thing that will ever keep us truly safe and truly joyous: your precious presence. In the name of your Son, we pray. Amen.

Primitive Hymn Anonymous sung to "All Saints New" the tune of "The Son of God Goes Forth to War"

What poor, despised company
Of travelers are these,
Who walk in yonder narrow way,
Along the rugged maze?
Ah! these are of a royal line,
All children of a King,
Heirs of immortal crowns divine;
And lo! for joy they sing.

Why do they, then, appear so mean,
And why so much despised?
Because of their rich robes unseen
The world is not apprized.
But why keep they that narrow road,
That rugged, thorny maze?
Why, that's the way their Leader trod,
They love and keep His ways.

> Why do they shun the pleasing path
> That worldlings love so well?
> Because that is the road to death,
> The open road to hell.
> What! is there then no other road
> To Salem's happy ground?
> Christ is the only way to God,
> No other can be found.

Egotism

A Reading
Proverbs 26:12

A Meditation
It is easy to see where the word egotism comes from. Before Freud made ego a technical term for part of the personality, it was a good solid Latin word meaning the first person "I." Over the last few years, there has been a tussle in the Christian church over the heavy use of the word "I" in the new songs the body of Christ sings. However, the briefest look at the Psalms will tell you that that word was very important in the life of the Hebrew community. Still, many people in our denomination take a dim view of all of the first-person language in our newer songs, saying that in their praise and confessions, they do not communicate the praise and the confession of the whole community.

So now I was dreadfully confused. How can we criticize the newer songs coming out of Christianity for being "I" centered when the oldest songs sung to God, the Psalms, couch their praise and confession in terms of the first person as well?

A few years ago, I attended a continuing education event and the presenter was an Old Testament professor, so I took the opportunity to pose her this problem. She told me that none of the songs, new, old, or very old, were the problem. In our society today, we simply do not understand the corporate I. The corporate I. I have to confess, I stood there rather stupidly, and therefore, making her point, repeating out loud, more than once, "the corporate I." Proving that at the very least, this particular modern person did not understand "the corporate I." Well, I was rescued. Last Thursday, at our midweek Bible Study, the text of Exodus gave me the opportunity to mention this "corporate I" business.

It seemed to confuse them not at all. We are all confessing that we believe and hope for the same things, but we are not assuming the right to confess the belief and hope of anyone else. I found as I always do, great understanding in our folks that come together on Thursday mornings. The more I thought about it, the more it became clear to me that not only do people have the opportunity to praise and confess their faith individually while singing with other Christians; the community is strengthened by the remembrance that God loves each one of us individually.

I am considering emailing that Old Testament professor and telling her that I have a whole class room full of people who have a perfect understanding of the "corporate I." I believe that even though Peter has taken it on the chin for the last 2,000 years, I believe he too understood the "corporate I." But he also had the gift from God of self-love: not only the ordinary human instinct to survive, but also that wonderful gift of self-love that comes whether we have a community that upholds it or not.

For this reason, we must work together, as a Christian community to uphold our individual member's gifts of self-love and not tear each other down. Peter had this gift and because of it, he acted and spoke when others would not or could not. The only time he did not was when he finally denied his Savior.

Pastor: Let us pray:
Congregation: Teach us, dear God, that we are not alone and that you have placed us in a world of people who need our example and whose help we need. Help us, God of all, to cheat ourselves of none of your blessings. In the name of your Son, we pray. Amen.

Impulsive

A Reading
Proverbs 29:20

A Meditation
Broken down into its roots, the word impulsive means to push before. This makes a lot of sense because one who is impulsive pushes before he or she has time to really think about it. These are the non-looking leapers we hear so much about. We see this in almost everything the Bible tells us about Peter. It shows up in the stories of the transfiguration, the walking on water business, and most terribly, in Peter's denial of his Lord.

Impulsiveness is a trait I fear I share with Peter. However, I have to confess that over the years it is something I have come to rely on more than reject as something that causes me trouble. I believe the same is true with Peter. It is pretty clear that he not only got into trouble when he tried water walking, he also looked just plain stupid. And because of his impulsiveness, he sounded like a babbling fool at our Lord's transfiguration. But his impulsiveness also kept him from being at his Lord's side when he denied him in the courtyard of the temple the night before Jesus died. But you have to ask yourself if he would have been the lion of faith that he was without all of those experiences.

Impulsiveness is a gift from God without which many things would not be done and many would not hear the good news. While it is true that the things for which Peter is best known shows us the negative side of impulsiveness, it is impulsiveness that made use of Peter's egotism and ended Peter's fear.

There are going to be times in our lives as Christians when we are weighed down by our fear. And it is only going to be our impulsiveness that will set us free to push out into the rest of the world before we have a chance to think about it. Before long, the lovely gift of self-love will be overshadowed by the darker gift of survival and unlike our dear friend Peter, we will not act, we will not speak out. Our Lord knows, as he knew with Peter, that we will deny him. Our impulsiveness is one of the gifts we have to set us free from our fear, and with Peter, to act and to speak on behalf of the world.

Offering

The Prayers of the People

The Lord's Prayer

Closing Hymn
"O Sacred Head, Now Wounded"

THE THIRD MIDWEEK SERVICE

The Witness of Caiaphas, High Priest
John 11:44-53; Matthew 26:57-66

Opening Hymn
"In the Cross of Christ I Glory"

The Witness
You'd think I would be past all of this. After all, if a person is the high priest, he should be able to make an assessment and stick by it. Usually I can, but not this time. All the way around, this time was different. I didn't think so at first. He seemed like just another troublemaker. He had all the characteristics: the ability to attract the big crowds with the flashy miracles and the charismatic personality. People I trust kept telling me that there was more to this one. But I figured it was just wishful thinking.

After all, people had started to claim that he was the Messiah finally come. Who wouldn't want to believe that? But, I'm afraid that for those of us who just barely manage to believe in the promise of the coming Messiah at all, it's a bit of a stretch to imagine that God would send his Anointed One in the person of a poor, ignorant man from the hill country or into this traitorous generation. I gave him the benefit of the doubt, though. Even more than that, for one fleeting moment I let myself wonder... and I have to tell you, for that one moment, I felt like my world was turning upside down.

I don't even think it had as much to do with the fact that I wanted to believe in him as it had to do with the amount of energy I had expended with regard to him. You see, I have never condoned murder of any kind in my whole life. But, you'd really have to understand what we've been up against here. We have been striving to live as faithful Jews

31

in a country in which striving to live as a faithful Jew is considered a waste of time because it doesn't get you anywhere with Rome. So all we have tried to do is strike a happy medium. We have continued to obey our God, despite the consequences to our income level, our social prestige, and even our personal safety. We have known that in order to continue God's work, we would need to keep from causing Rome trouble. Not that they care who or what we worship, they just want the tax money to keep flowing. And of course, this is something that this country rube, this Jesus person, was not sophisticated enough to understand. As I say, I am not one to ever condone murder, but we gave this guy warning after warning. For three years, we asked him to watch what he said, to keep from undermining the elders and the priests, to stop giving Rome ammunition, but he would not listen. He continued to threaten our already-shaky relationship with Rome. So, it came down to a choice, either we shut him up, or we let Rome shut the synagogues down. And that was no choice.

In the face of our sacred duty, to prevent the death of 2,000 years of devotion, of tradition, of remembrance, one life seemed a small price to be paid. The price didn't feel small that night. I found myself hoping that he was the Messiah. I almost begged him to say that he was. But he just stood there. When he finally did speak, it didn't make any sense. What he said was guaranteed to send him to the cross. I knew then that he was just another crazy out for his moment in the sun. But at that same moment, I felt my faith in the coming Messiah vanish.

Opening Prayer
Pastor: Let us pray:
Congregation: One and only God, in you alone do we place our trust, or at least try to. Forgive us, Savior God, when we place more trust in the fleeting, false, and finite

things of this world than we do in the love that broke down the gates of death. Break our habit of clinging to that which is second best when you are extending to us that which is eternal and the very best. In the name of your Son, we pray. Amen.

Arrogance

A Reading
Isaiah 2:12-19

A Meditation
Arrogance. From the Latin, this word means to "not ask." *Rogo* means to ask, as in interrogate and in many cases, the addition of the letter "a" in front of another Latin word makes it a negative. There are few better examples of arrogance than Caiaphas. And that arrogance is part of the reason he held the position he did.

A quick look around at our society and its leadership will tell you that it takes tough skin to survive as a leader these days. Not just political but all kinds of leaders: teachers, bosses, parents, pastors all field criticism. Maybe they always did. As high priest, Caiaphas outranked just about every other religious or political leader, and this had to be particularly difficult time to rule as a Jew. Jews were not in charge. They were given the illusion of sovereignty.

It would be like living in any of the former Yugoslavian countries during the Soviet era. In many cases, these countries were given the illusion of control but not only were the really important decisions made by Russians, the really good, important, and lucrative jobs were reserved for Russians, even if they were working in what was called Belarus, the Ukraine, or something else.

This is the same thing the Jews faced in Caiaphas' day. Any Jewish tradition and reading of what we call the Old Testament, any prayers made to our God were made possible by Caiaphas and people like them. All in all, Caiaphas must have been a pretty impressive guy. And let's face it, he has some pretty compelling reasons to be arrogant.

First of all, he must not appear to be weak, which he would were he to appear not to know all the answers. Any sign of weakness would have caused Rome concern. Plus, he must not second guess himself. No leader in his position could afford to doubt his decisions, at least publicly. Any parent knows that.

Well, in Caiaphas' case, multiply that pressure by 50,000 and we get some idea of the pressure he was under. But we see from our readings, he does ask questions, but we also see that his questions are more like accusations. We also see something else in his statements. We see fleeting and nearly unrecognizable hope.

Pastor: Let us pray:
Congregation: Father above, you are and always have been far beyond our understanding. Help us to live in fearful joy within the bounds of our lack of understanding because of your blessing of faith. Forgive us when we cease to trust you or consider you someone with whom we need only reckon at our deaths. Rather give us the courage to approach you day by day, moment by moment. In the name of your Son, we pray. Amen.

Primitive Hymn Isaac Watts to tune of "O God Our Help in Ages Past"

>   I'm not ashamed to own my Lord,
>   Or to defend His cause;
>   Maintain the honor of His Word,
>   The glory of His cross.

> Jesus, my God! I know his Name,
> his Name is all my trust;
> Nor will he put my soul to shame,
> Nor let my hope be lost.
>
> Firm as his throne his promise stands,
> And he can well secure
> What I've committed to his hands
> Till the decisive hour.
>
> Then will he own my worthless name
> Before his Father's face,
> And in the new Jerusalem
> Appoint my soul a place.

Contradiction

A Reading
Luke 11:37-44

A Meditation
Contradiction is another word that we can understand more completely by taking it apart. Literally, it means words against. *Dict* meaning word as in dictionary and *contra* as in against. I thought of this work when I looked at the statements Caiaphas made to and regarding Jesus. Both these statements are used by God.

The first is a prophecy as John tells us, but Caiaphas thinks of it as a surgical removal of a dangerous element. Even the way he states it makes me believe this was not a decision with which he was comfortable. He says, "Don't you know it is better for one person to die for the people than for the whole nation to be destroyed?" But before he says that he becomes angry because the people around him do not understand the stakes. It seems that they are more worried about their own following… worried that the people will follow Jesus and not them. Only Caiaphas sees the stakes as they are. What a contradiction. Kill someone to save the lives of others. But when you look at it, Caiaphas' life, in fact the lives of all the leaders in Israel, must have seemed like a contradiction.

Defending Judaism by placating the Romans. Why should this surprise us? Aren't our lives a lot of the times, just the same? Don't we find ourselves trying to placate the world, trying to look like the rest of the world? And it will get worse and worse. All of the reasons people used to come to church are no longer in force. For years, going to church made you look good. For years, going to church was a good way to get ahead in business. What a contradiction that was. Now, those of us who go to church come because we have no choice in the matter. Or rather, we have decided to have no choice in the matter. Church is now the place at which we feel the most direct link to God. We need to rid ourselves of the contradictions. The other statement Caiaphas made comes at the very end of our text.

We need no more witnesses. I think that he was crushingly disappointed by what must have seemed to him to be Jesus' blasphemous response. He decided to put aside any concerns he had and defend what he knew. And Jesus died.

Pastor: Let us pray:
Congregation: Lord, when we face our confusing and perplexing world, help us to remember that you have claimed us. When we feel the need to find our footing anywhere but in your love, defend us from our own foolishness. In the name of your Son, we pray. Amen.

Self-Satisfaction
A Reading
Luke 18:9-14

A Meditation

Self-Satisfaction. In every case I have ever seen or personally experienced, self-satisfaction could more appropriately be the second step to self-destruction. The first step is self-delusion. We have already seen Caiaphas do just that. The moment he sold his soul to Rome, his trust in Yahweh vanished. He had knelt down to an idol as surely as his ancestors did when they bowed down to the golden calf in the desert. We see the smug way he sends Jesus to his death, and we realize he is not really even worshiping Rome. He is worshiping the same god we all worship on a regular basis, whether we are Christians, Moslems, Jews, Hindus, Buddhists, or agnostics. He was worshiping not so much himself, but his own safety. When we do that, when we decide to save our money and not share it with the needy, when we opt to go bowling instead of giving blood, when we decide to catch up on work at the house instead of helping to clean the church, we are protecting ourselves. We are protecting our futures through our financial stability, our social standing, or our family happiness. God wants us to be happy and safe. But God wants us to understand what real safety is. Safety is understanding that we live our lives knowing that heaven is our home. This means there is nothing we need to hang onto. To do anything else is to believe that we have control over our lives. Such an attitude is self-delusion. The only way to keep a delusion alive is to feed it. That is what Caiaphas did.

First of all, if you will notice, he asked his colleagues: What do you think? Now, why should the high priest do such a thing? Why would the high priest have to ask? I thought he was arrogant. Well, probably he thought it was a rhetorical question needing no answer. I think he was probably feeding his own self-delusion until it became self-satisfaction. With that, he denied himself Jesus' intervention in his life and sent himself down the path of self-destruction. We must never deny ourselves Jesus. We must do whatever it takes to ask, to trust, and to rejoice.

Offering

The Prayers of the People

The Lord's Prayer

Closing Hymn
"O Sacred Head, Now Wounded"

THE FOURTH MIDWEEK SERVICE

The Witness of Herod, Tetrarch of Jerusalem
Matthew 14:1-11; Luke 23:8-12; Acts 12:1-4, 20-23

Opening Hymn
"O God, Our Help in Ages Past"

The Witness
I am king of Galilee. When my father died, I took over in his place.

I was the obvious choice. I came with the recommendation of my good friend, Caesar Tiberius, emperor of Rome. That idiot Pilate said I was a spy for Tiberius. He simply was not sophisticated enough to understand the mind of royalty. I was the best and most trusted friend of Emperor Tiberius.

Speaking of total lack of sophistication, all the trouble started when this rube, this Jesus person showed up here. I had never met him, but I heard much about him. Everyone had. I wanted very much to meet him... to see if what they were saying about him was true.

This charlatan, the one telling everyone he is a doctor, this Luke, wrote that I was out to kill Jesus. These people, why am I surrounded by imbeciles? That simply is not true! I had nothing against him. I just wanted to keep peace in Galilee, and he was causing such an uproar. I just hoped he would move on somewhere else.

Ah, yes. I remember the day he came before me very well. I was in Jerusalem for the Passover. Pilate knew I was there. When the leaders of the temple brought charges against him, Pilate was too much of a coward to deal with him. He sent him to me. I was glad to meet this Jesus face-to-face. I wanted to know if all the outrageous things they claimed about him were true. That he was a miracle worker, that he was a healer, and that he raised a man from the dead. Some claimed that he was the Messiah that was to come. I wanted to hear from him to see if any of it was true.

I was not at all surprised to find that he was an imposter. He gave me no proof for any of the things they said about him, and he was insolent and rude.

He didn't even answer any of my questions. I gave him an opportunity to prove himself. I was curious. I'm a Jew. He was one of my people. If he was a miracle worker, if he was the Messiah, all he had to do was say so. Really, I was giving him an opportunity to show the world who he was. All he had to do was show me. But he didn't even answer me. He didn't even speak. Ridiculous! It was a waste of my time.

Here I was in Jerusalem to celebrate the Passover and I get called out to listen to this silence! this impostor! all because Pilate didn't have the guts to deal with him himself.

So I sent him back to Pilate, of course. I told him to take care of his own dirty work. We all know why the temple priests wanted him out of the way. He was popular; a threat to their power. He was turning the people against them, and Jerusalem was Pilate's jurisdiction. Let him take care of Jesus.

As far as I was concerned, he had committed no crime, except he pretended to be something he wasn't. So, you can't pin his blood on my hands. I told you, it was Pilate. He put Jesus to death.

Opening Prayer
Pastor: Let us pray:
Congregation: For thine is the kingdom, and the power, and the glory forever and ever. Amen. So we pray. You are all we need. Remind us of this, sweet holy God, when we try to be more than we are. Help us to remember that through you, we are far more than we ever thought we could be. In the name of your Son, we pray. Amen.

Cipher

A Reading
Psalm 49

A Meditation
A cipher, or a place holder, that is what Herod was. However, a place holder, cipher, or zero, whether in politics or in mathematics, can still cause a lot of trouble. I remember an old *Beverly Hillbillies* show where Jethro is learning arithmetic. He said that if you put, what he called an aught, which was a corruption of the word naught or nothing, he said if you put aughts in front of a number it didn't mean a thing, but if you put them behind a number, "Them aughts is dynamite." He was right about that.

Just because Herod was functionally powerless did not mean he did not cause plenty of damage. Now before we go any further with this, perhaps we should, as we have this whole Lenten season, figure out what another word means. The word we must direct our attention to is Herod's title: Tetrach. Tetracycline in an antibiotic made up of four different elements and the Tetragrammaton is where we get the name Yahweh. Yahweh is the sound of the four Hebrew letters that go into the sentence "I am who I am," the name God gave Moses.

Most of us think of words beginning with *qua*, such as quartet when we think of the number four. And that is true in Latin, but in Greek it is *tetra*. Therefore a tetrarch is the ruler of a fourth of a province. As a consequence, it seems that such a one would not be a cipher or a mere placeholder. And that would be true, were it not for Rome. Anything he did could be overruled, or worse, simply ignored by Pilate and the rest of the population of Israel who knew that Pilate held the military, and the high priest held the palace guard. Herod descended from once-mighty kings, who, bit by bit, became more and more spoiled and pampered until they had no fortitude or will of their own. Everything we see Herod do, we see him do for his own enhancement. Nor does he bother to think of the consequences of his act. His story is fundamentally sad because it is one of someone who, while he may not understand it completely, knows deep in his heart that his existence, his pampered, luxurious existence, has no meaning.

Pastor: Let us pray:
Congregation: Heaven is our home, dear Lord. Because of this, we are neither empty nor insignificant. Help us to use the wondrous power the gospel gives us, to bring your will to the earth. In the name of your Son, we pray. Amen.

Primitive Hymn by Isaac Watts sung to "Woodworth" the tune of "Just as I Am"

>My spirit looks to God alone;
>My rock and refuge is his throne;
>In all my fears, in all my straits,
>My soul on his salvation waits.
>
>Trust him, ye saints, in all your ways,
>Pour out your hearts before his face:
>When helpers fail, and foes invade,
>God is our all-sufficient aid.
>
>False are the men of high degree,
>The baser sort are vanity;
>Laid in the balance, both appear
>Light as a puff of empty air.
>
>Make not increasing gold your trust,
>Nor set your hearts on glitt'ring dust

Why will you grasp the fleeting smoke,
And not believe what God has spoke?

Once has his awful voice declared,
Once and again my ears have heard,
All power is his eternal due;
He must be feared and trusted too.

For sovereign power reigns not alone,
Grace is a partner of the throne:
Thy grace and justice, mighty Lord,
Shall well divide our last reward.

Vanity

A Reading
Psalm 36:1-4

A Meditation
In our society, we tend to think of someone who is vain as someone who is conceited. That is a legitimate understanding only because to be vain in that way is to think only of your physical appearance. Actually, the word vanity, as used famously in the book of Ecclesiastes, means emptiness. In fact, the actual Hebrew word used in Ecclesiastes means vapor.

But the word "vain" has an interesting history. It is a corruption of the word wane, as in the moon. It waxes and wanes. It becomes smaller when it wanes. To wane is to become nothing.

Poor Herod understood that he was nothing. Therefore, he was vain, always caring about appearances. Now, I have a much different understanding of this difficulty than I did when I was younger. When I was young, strong, and stupid, I had contempt for people who, at least, to my eyes, cared only for appearances and did not seem to focus on reality. That was before I realized that for most of us, most of the time, appearance is reality. We can say you can't judge a book by its cover until you are blue in the face, but that is what most of us do most of the time. Even when we are thinking about things, we tend to resort to preconceived ideas and make snap judgments. Whether you are a politician, pastor, or parent, every leader knows that it is not just improprieties, the bad decisions, the injudicious acts that are the problem, it is the appearance of all those things.

Knowing he was nothing, it was even more important to Herod that he make a very good first impression. And there are one or two ways to make that happen: either look really good physically or seem all powerful. We don't have any data to confirm or deny the first, but our own Bible gives us plenty of examples of the second. It is when we are desperate to appear to be something other than we are that we end up committing those improprieties, those bad decisions, those injudicious acts.

Herod did not understand who Jesus was. Had he, he would have learned that there was no need to pretend to be anything other than he was.

Pastor: Let us pray:
Congregation: Dear God in heaven, what can we say to you that you do not already know? What can we give you over which you do not already have complete control? We are humbled as we come before you. But in that humility we discover an unexpected gift: We discover that we are loved. In the name of your Son, we pray. Amen.

Delusion

A Reading
James 4:13-17

A Meditation
A donkey was owned and abused by an old western prospector. For months on end, this poor donkey walked, pulled, ate, and slept with a tremendous load on his back. In fact, he had borne the heavy load for so long that not only had he become seriously swaybacked with the load, he had forgotten that it was there. One day, the prospector and his donkey traveled to a village so that the prospector could cash in his dust and re-supply. There the donkey had occasion to visit with the other donkeys in the same business. The first donkey he spoke with said, "That's quite a load you have there." To this, the other donkey replied, "What load?"

By the time Herod was around my age, right around fifty, delusion was the only comfort he had left. Ten years later, at the time of his death he was positively barking, claiming to be God. He was completely deluded.

Now once again, it seems that we have an interesting word here. *Ludere* in the Latin means to play. De- can mean undone but it can also mean under. Someone who is deluded has been taken under or sucked into their play life. Such was clearly the case of Herod. He was lost in his own world, even though Christ had come among him to bring him into God's complete safety.

All of us, are ciphers. We are all vain. We are all delusional. Except when we realize that we have one thing and one thing only on which we can rely: the love of God. Through the love of God, we have purpose, we have unassailable dignity, and we have an unquestionable future. All those things Herod was so desperate to procure. All these things, our Savior gave us on the cross free for the taking. All these things our Savior offers us day after day. All these things we can share with the world.

The Offering

The Prayers of the People

The Lord's Prayer

Closing Hymn
"O Sacred Head, Now Wounded" No. 117

THE FIFTH MIDWEEK

The Witness of Pontius Pilate, Roman Governor of Israel
John 18:28-38; Matthew 27:15-26

Opening Hymn
"Rock of Ages"

The Witness
I was the supreme military ruler for Caesar Tiberius in charge of the province of Judea for Rome. The Jews of the territory had their laws they said were given to them by their God. But the only true law for them was Roman law. I was the true judge and final authority for the law. Now, most of the Jews understood this and even appreciated the progress that Rome represented.

That was true about most of their leaders as well, but after this occurrence, I found I wanted less and less to do with them. I saw men I had grown to respect, particularly Caiaphas, doing things I never would have imagined he could have done.

This man was innocent. The Jews brought him to me on trumped-up charges. They wanted him out of the way. They wanted me to do it for them.

So? Why should I care? What's one pious Jew to me? They wanted him killed. They must have had their reasons.

Still, I found that he had done nothing for which to kill him. They brought him to me saying he was a threat to Rome; saying he was going to overthrow our Roman rule.

But then I came up with a plan. I sent him to that puppet king of theirs. I thought that if they wanted him killed, let their king do it. But, like the coward he was, he sent him back to me.

He knew as well as I did that Jesus was no threat to us. But, apparently, he was a threat to the Jews. Jerusalem was full of people. And everyone had an opinion about this man... So I gave him the chance to speak for himself. I asked him if he was the king of the Jews. He answered in riddles. "You say that I am," but I never said that. When I gave him the chance to answer his accusers, he was silent... wouldn't say anything. Then I asked if there was anyone who would speak for him. No one would.

Except for my wife, but she's always telling me about this dream and that dream. I don't pay attention to her ravings anyway.

Don't you see? I really had no choice. I gave him every chance but he never defended himself. So, I took advantage of their festival. I offered to free a prisoner for them. I figured if he was so popular, the crowd would want him freed. But they yelled, "Crucify him." They asked for Barabbas; not Jesus.

The Jews wanted it. They all yelled for it. Nobody spoke against them.

So in the end, I complied. But at least I was able to humiliate them in revenge for the difficult position they had put me in. I put a sign over him when he was crucified. It said, "King of the Jews." The Jews hated it. I enjoyed it! In a way, this Jesus was more fit to be king of the Jews than any of them. I am not saying I felt real good about it, but if I hadn't, I guarantee a lot more people would have died.

There is an old legend hanging around that I committed suicide. Well, I'm not going to confirm that but if I did, who could blame me? This crazy man's death was laid at my feet. I gave him every chance to be free. He wouldn't defend himself. It was as if he could care less whether he lived or died. I just did what everyone wanted.

Now I understand that my name is mentioned more often in your century than any other Roman, even Caesar, and all because I just tried to do what I thought was right at the time.

Opening Prayer
Pastor: Let us pray:
Congregation: God of the day and the night, that which we see and that which is hidden, forgive our desire to trust only what can be verified. Help us to trust in the one who has created us and given us the sacred task of caring for it. Forgive us when our courage fails, and we leave off loving ourselves enough to trust in you. In the name of your Son, we pray. Amen.

Irresolution

A Reading
Hosea 7:8-12

A Meditation
Picking a word to describe Pilate was difficult. Mostly because so many words would fit, and I admit that I chose irresolute because it had the most interesting history. This word is one of many words that comes from the Latin word *solve* meaning to loosen or to break up into its component parts. This is where we get our words solution, solve, dissolute, dissolve, as well as irresolute. These words mean many things and not all of them relate to each other. But in a way they all hang together in that they all relate to somehow taking something apart or putting it back together. In this word we find two prefixes, but were we to simply look at the word resolute, indicating a willingness, in fact, an eagerness to take a stand, we get a pretty good picture of Pilate, if we use the prefix *ir* indicating the negative of resolute. He was by no means eager to take a stand. He was resentful that he was placed in the position he found himself. He was as much a victim of circumstance as the other people who lived in

Jerusalem at this time and he was as guilty of Jesus' death as we are.

Looking at his situation, I suspect he made the wisest, or at least, the most politically expedient decision he could have made at the time. Truly, had Jesus been released, two things, at the very least, would have happened.

Eventually, we human beings would have found a way to kill Jesus, not only because we believe that was God's will, but also because we could not have stood his perfection and the longer Jesus lived on earth, the bloodier his death would have been. Also, the Jewish leadership may well have withdrawn their support for Pilate. They would have signed their death warrant to do so, but humans being as self-destructive as we know them to be, I don't believe that would have stopped them and more blood than Jesus' and Judas' would have been shed.

In a way, calling Pilate irresolute is unfair. In fact, to link his actions with any word whose root is *solve*, meaning to break up into its component parts, the famous Aristotelian logic that claims you cannot understand any idea until you have broken it down into its component parts, is unfair. The idea was and is beyond Pilate's or our understanding. Pilate was irresolute in the same way we are irresolute when we doubt God by worrying, and we have the resurrection, our absolute freedom in which to find great hope. Pilate, being who and what he was, made the best decision he could based on the circumstances.

Prayer
Pastor: Let us pray:
Congregation: Trust in you is our only weapon in our struggle against fear, dear Lord. Sweeten our lives with your messengers of faith. Open our hearts to the words, the embraces, and the healing work all done in obedience to your Son in whose name we pray. Amen.

Primitive Hymn to "Martyrdom" the tune of "Alas! And Did My Savior Bleed" Isaac Watts

> God of my life, look gently down,
> Behold the pains I feel;
> But I am dumb before thy throne,
> Nor dare dispute thy will.
>
> I'm but a sojourner below,
> As all my fathers were;
> May I be well prepared to go,
> When I the summons hear.
>
> But if my life be spared awhile,
> Before my last remove,
> Thy praise shall be my business still,
> And I'll declare thy love.

Capitulate

A Reading
Psalm 135:15-18

A Meditation
Now, here is an interesting word. Its Latin root, which is only about 1,000 years old itself, is a legal term, *capitulare*. That isn't even the root. The real root is *capo*, as in head, like the old Mafia term and the word captain. But *capitulare* is the word used for the heading of chapters on legal documents. It has evolved into a word that means what the loser of a law suit does when he signs off on the decision. He states that he yields up whatever he has tried to gain or maintain. This high powered and very negative word comes from the same place we get the important but far more innocuous words like cap or capital, both indicating the head or the top. Clearly, capitulating is something Pilate did.

But he didn't just yield up Jesus. He yielded up his relationship with his wife, he yielded up his up his integrity, he yielded up any regard he had for his Jewish colleagues, and he yielded up his respect for Roman Law, still the greatest legal system in the Western world, the system most Western countries use, including our own. Pilate yielded up all these treasured things when he yielded to the Jewish authorities concerning Jesus. You see, that is the problem with capitulating to the world over against the will of God. The will of the world will drag so many of God's gifts away from us. When we decide one aspect of God's will, one gift of God, or one of God's children is not worth defending, it's open season on anything else. Now, if our God was an angry, vengeful, and fearsome God it would be one thing, but our God is not. The temptation to capitulate to the world should be very easy to avoid. But we can see the world. We cannot see God. Therefore, we must remember who God is in our lives and in the lives of those who have gone before us. This is absolutely critical, because we have a responsibility to the people who come after us.

It is an axiom in the worlds of business, politics, and religion that to capitulate is to perpetuate. If we yield to a wasteful, careless, poorly conceived, or dangerous practice, you insure its continuance. God knows, I have seen that at the After School program. It is very difficult to make kids behave if in the past they have gotten away with bad behavior. We can all think of times in which this is true in our lives as family members, business people, or members of a community. But here again, in this specific situation, it does not really apply to Pilate. He had no way of knowing that the bad behavior he was being forced to give in to had been part of God's plan. He yielded in order to maintain law and order, not realizing that the maker of all laws had been in control of the situation from the beginning.

Pastor: Let us pray:
Congregation: Teach us to love ourselves. It should be so easy. We are loved by you. What greater evidence of worth could there be that to be loved by the creator, the redeemer of the world? For such is your love for us, dear heavenly parent. In the name of your Son, we pray. Amen.

Despair

A Reading
Isaiah 59:9-21

A Meditation
This sad word comes from the same word from which we derive the word for our breath: respiration. Because, truly, where there's life, there's hope. And where there is life, there is breath. Clearly, by the end of this experience, Pilate had lost all hope. He had watched everything he cherished being brought into question. So, even though he drew breath, he probably drew no hope.

Had we not sinned, Jesus would have had no need to come. Had we not sinned, Judas would not have despaired and taken his life. Had we not sinned, Pilate would not have needed to betray everything he trusted. Had we not sinned, our lives would be peaceful and without pain. But we sinned. Instead of allowing us to fall prey to our own selfishness and self-destruction, Jesus came. Jesus became one of us. Jesus gave his life for us. Jesus cracked death's door wide open so that we need not despair.

Offering

The Prayers of the People

The Lord's Prayer

Closing Hymn
"O Sacred Head, Now Wounded"

MAUNDY THURSDAY SERVICE

Opening Hymn
"O Jesus, I Have Promised" No. 503

Opening Litany
Isaiah 65:17-20, 24
Behold, I will create new heavens and a new earth. The former things will not be remembered,
nor will they come to mind.
But be glad and rejoice forever in what I will create,
for I will create Jerusalem to be a delight and its people a joy.
I will rejoice over Jerusalem and take delight in my people;
the sound of weeping and of crying will be heard in it no more.
Before they call I will answer;
while they are still speaking I will hear.
The wolf and the lamb will feed together,
and the lion will eat straw like the ox.

The First Reading
Exodus 12:1-14

Service of Public Confession and Absolution
Pastor: Today as we near the end of Lent's dark journey, the lengthening days have given us the time we need to look deeply into ourselves and in our deepest needs. As the days have warmed, we have felt the safety of God's loving embrace as we faced the reality of our sinful states. As we continue throughout our lives, to enter into God's grace, we are upheld by God's word of promise. We declare this to ourselves, to God, and to each other as we say the words that reveal our failing and declare our faith. Let us pray.

Left Side: When we fail to bring your love into consideration or when we slip into apathy or despair about the world.
Right side: When we fail to take strength and courage from the example of your Son.
Left Side: When by our inaction, we allow injustice, greed, selfishness, and even cruelty to go unchecked.
Right side: When by our inaction, we allow your truth to go unspoken and undefended, ignored, and mocked.
All: Though we are unworthy, Lord, forgive us.
Left Side: When with our apathy and despair, we fall into dangerous, abusive, and destructive habits,
Right side: or allow our hopelessness to turn into cynicism or the deadly desire for power, wealth, or other forms of earthly corruptible security.
All: Though we are unworthy, Lord, forgive us.
Left Side: When in our weakness and fear, we allow ourselves to be dragged down into a place in which we see no way to live that does not involve sinful behavior,
Right-side: and perhaps find our strength and our courage in sin instead of in your goodness.
All: Though we are unworthy, Lord, forgive us.
Left Side: When we find profane power and treacherous security in acts of injustice, greed, selfishness, and cruelty.
Right side: And allow others to pay the cost for that power and security
All: Though we are unworthy, Lord, forgive us.
Left Side: When we neglect the truth that your Son died to show us, when we abuse those who try to spread that truth with words and actions with our fearful doubt and our lack of support,
Right side: when we show the world how little your love really means to us.
All: Though we are unworthy, Lord, forgive us.
We stand before you, dear Lord, knowing that you have already forgiven us. Help us to listen as you speak your

word of acceptance, your word of mercy, and your word of redemption.
All: In the name of your Son we pray. Amen.

The Gospel Verse
Pastor: "Do not store up for yourselves treasures on earth, where moth and rust destroy, and where thieves break in and steal. But store up for yourselves treasures in heaven, where moth and rust do not destroy, and where thieves do not break in and steal."
Congregation: For where your treasure is, there your heart will be also.

The Gospel Lesson
Matthew 26:17-29

Primitive Hymn by Isaac Watts sung to "New Britain" tune of "Amazing Grace"

>When I can read my title clear
>To mansions in the skies,
>I bid farewell to every fear,
>And wipe my weeping eyes.
>
>Should earth against my soul engage,
>And hellish darts be hurled,
>Then I can smile at Satan's rage,
>And face a frowning world.
>
>Let cares, like a wild deluge come,
>And storms of sorrow fall!
>May I but safely reach my home,
>My God, my heav'n, my All.

> There shall I bathe my weary soul
> In seas of heav'nly rest,
> And not a wave of trouble roll,
> Across my peaceful breast.

Homily

Everyone who has ever gone out of their way to try to do something special for a family member, friend, or coworker knows the disappointment and perhaps even heartbreak that follows when that special effort is not appreciated. Every responsible teacher knows the frustration of working very hard at a lesson plan only to have his or her students roll their eyes and ignore them. Every employee who as ever gone the extra mile to earn their boss' respect knows the irritation of being taken for granted.

Now, as mature adults, we know that disappointment, frustration, and irritation are a part of the life of the individual who takes their relationship with the rest of the world seriously. As hard as we try, there will always be people around who don't show their appreciation and, once in a while, everyone forgets to do, say, or notice the right thing and people's feelings get hurt. It may seem to the Christian that they are more on the receiving end of this sort of behavior than anyone else. Now the Bible never tells us the way to avoid being disappointed, frustrated, or irritated by life and the people around us. In fact, our Lord makes it clear that he expects such experiences.

The Bible does, however, give us a way to place these feelings in perspective. These words are in our gospel lesson for this evening. Our Lord gave his flesh for us, for the world, a world that did not appreciate his sacrifice, in fact, reviled it. Even his own people, those who cling to the salvation made possible by our Lord' sacrifice, routinely take it for granted. But in so doing, he did not just risk being disappointed, frustrated, or irritated. He didn't risk at all. The sacrifice of his flesh was a sure thing.

But, still, his sacrifice was extreme. All of the sacrifices that we make for each other and for the world cannot help us to see what our Lord's sacrifice felt like. We could never suffer as much as he did because we could never have given up as much as he did. Not only did he give us his flesh. Who knows how many people have given up their lives for the people and the ideas that they loved? But it was not just this life that he gave up. He had given up his life in heaven to live among us and by taking on this life, his precious flesh became the bread of heaven. This bread of heaven fuels us for eternal life. Unless we take that bread, unless we allow our Lord's sacrifice into our lives, there is nothing else that can fuel us for eternity. Nothing.

Many people view the film *Cool Hand Luke* as a modern-day story of Christ. Nothing could be further from the truth. Even though the character tries to do what is right for the people around him, eventually, he fails. Cool Hand Luke is on a southern chain gang. The prison is run by a pompous warden assisted by a menacing captain who never speaks and whose expressions are hidden by a pair of mirrored sunglasses. The inmates suffer at the hands of these two men until Cool Hand Luke arrives as an inmate. Luke defies the guards and their inhumanity in many unique ways. He gives life and hope to the inmates, and they all live vicariously through him. But every man has his breaking point and finally even Luke is broken. Luke is stretched out on a table with arms out to his sides as other inmates gather around after a severe beating. They try to lift his spirits by encouraging him to fight back, fight back for their sakes. At that point Luke cries out, "Quit feeding off me," and then passes out because of his wounds.

We cannot feed off other human beings, but we can feed off the one who is the bread of life. He is the only one who can feed us now and eternally. The reason Luke failed was that he was not focusing on the only one who could give him the strength he needed to continue to do what was right. Rather than being a modern-day depiction of the story of the life of Christ, Cool Hand Luke is the story of a man who is faced with and defeated by the disappointment, frustration, and irritation this life brings with it.

By welcoming into our lives the one who can feed us now and eternally, we can accept and even disregard the disappointment, frustration, and irritation that so often accompanies Christian life. When we feel that the world does not appreciate what we have to give them, we are right. But that doesn't mean we should stop sharing what we have.

Have you ever noticed someone with some really good news? Very often, they tell everyone who will listen. How often are they convinced to stop sharing the good news simply because the people they are telling are not listening. Eventually, it happens, but in most cases, it takes a while. Our news is too good not to share.

And our Lord died so that it would be ours to share. Mother Cabrini, the first American citizen to be canonized, after whom the once hopeful and now infamous Cabrini Green Neighborhood in Chicago is named, was the youngest of thirteen children, born to a family in northern Italy. Her parents died when she was two. And at the age of eight she announced, "I am going to be a missionary to China when I grow up." Her brothers and sisters laughed at her. "You can't be a missionary," they said. "The church only uses men, not women. Anyway, you are too sickly." But she was determined, and when she finished her formal education, which would have qualified her to become a teacher in an order, the Catholic church refused to take her. "You are too weak," they said. And she was. She didn't even weigh a hundred pounds, and she spit blood all the time. But her strong will overcompensated for her weak body. "I'll take my case to the Pope," she declared. "Sister Cabrini," The Pope's voice was firm as he looked down on this frail, determined nun, "the church does not send women to be missionaries to China or any place." "Then, Holy Father," she responded, "I shall start an order for women only." "Agreed," the Pope returned, "providing you will go as a missionary to Italians in New York City."

Sister Frances Cabrini accepted the compromise. For months she waited on Ellis Island, still spitting blood. Finally, frustrated with the senseless delay, she appealed to the hierarchy of the Catholic church in New York. "Frankly, Sister," she was told, "you're too sickly. Go home!" Righteously indignant, she stamped her foot and rebuked the Archbishop. "Sir, I will not go home. I am at home here now." With that, the Archbishop gave in and let her stay.

Few people today know what New York was like at the turn of the century. Poor and homeless immigrants were wandering lonely, unloved, and lost in a new land. To them came this angel from God, and by 1916, through her beautiful love, over sixty houses had been founded, providing homes for the orphans and hospitals for the sick and the dying. We can share our good news by letting people know why we are willing to continue to be generous, open, and loving to people who neither appreciate it nor understand it. We know that our Lord died so that we could live a life free from fear, embraced in love, and sharing the news of our Lord's sacrifice.

The Offering

The Prayers of the People

Psalm 22

The Word of Institution

The Lord's Prayer

Post Communion Prayer
Pastor: We give you thanks Lord that you have welcomed us, unworthy as we are into your presence. Fill us with gratitude born of the knowledge of your Son's sacrifice and send us forth to understand the freedom and joy this sacrifice can mean.
Congregation: Amen.

Closing Hymn
"Were You There?" No. 92, vv. 1-3

The congregation will leave in silence.

GOOD FRIDAY

The Witness of the Crowd
Matthew 27:32-54

Opening Hymn
"Glory Be to Jesus"

Opening Prayer
Pastor: Let us pray:
Congregation: We are still the crowd, Lord Jesus, careless and perhaps even unaware that it was for us that you died. Turn us to you Lord. Turn us away from our own fears, our own greed, and our sick desire for belonging at any cost. Turn us to you, O Lord, and give us peace. Amen.

Desperation

A Reading
Mark 5:24-34

A Meditation
The word desperate comes from the same place the word despair comes from. They both indicate the place that hope is preparing to desert. On our Good Friday journey, we first see our Lord's greatest and most pervasive enemy, the crowd, nearly crushing him in their despair, in their desperation. Out of this pool of misery, we see that same hope reaching out in the form of a woman whom her society has cast off for twelve years. Because of her flow of blood, she should not even have been in the crowd to begin with. One of the saddest moments in the gospel, we realize that this woman has "heard" about Jesus. Unlike most sick people in the gospel, this poor woman had not been brought by a daughter

or a mother, or a neighbor or a niece. She had just heard about him. She had never even been told. This woman is a total outcast. Outcasts are largely the people who were drawn to Jesus. Because they had little power over their own lives, first of all because many of them were poor, and secondly because, as in the case of this woman, they had had to use many of their resources in order to regain their health, even if they wanted to, they couldn't have defended Jesus, so would have been his enemies. But in their desperation, like all the other people we have encountered this Lent, they are the enemies of Jesus because of the anger that comes from despair.

In 1986, a woman living in San Antonio, Texas, was diagnosed as having the AIDS virus after she received a blood transfusion. Eight years later, she took another AIDS test with a false name and discovered that a terrible mistake had been made and that she had never had the virus. This might have made her happy. But during those eight years, she had spent much time, energy, and money on cures. She was subjected to the terrible and exhausting side effects of drugs that were never necessary and, worst of all, she watched her two sons' anger change from rage to alienation and finally to desertion.

When we despair, we become our Lord's enemies. We become people who commit the sin Luther calls shameful. We need to be like the woman whose hope reached out to her Savior's cloak and claimed healing.

Pastor: Let us pray:
Congregation: Sweet Holy Jesus, teach us to cling to you and your almighty love. Steer us back to you so that we may find joy, purpose, courage, and peace in your love. Amen.

Avarice

A Reading
John 6:25-27

A Meditation
The word avarice comes from the Latin word for greed. And what we see in this text we have before us is not greed in the traditional sense, but it is greed, nonetheless. After Jesus had fed them, the crowd came to find Jesus. Their confusion at the beginning of the text is easy to explain. In every gospel, Jesus walks on water shortly after he feeds the multitude. This explains the confusion on the part of the crowd when they say, "Rabbi, when did you get here?" They literally don't know how he swung it. He didn't come across the lake as the crow flew but as the fish swum. But Jesus tells them that they came after him because they had had their fill of the loaves; not because they heard his message.

Recently on the radio, there was an exposé on prosperity preachers: preachers who preach that God wants us to be rich. The reporter did not take issue with these preachers' theology but rather how rich they got telling others God wants them to be rich. To preach such a thing is to entirely miss the point. By chasing after Jesus for another free meal is worse than buying a famous painting in order to have canvas in which to paint a sign announcing your garage sale.

It is to entirely miss the point and more terribly, it is to entirely miss the opportunity that Jesus has for us. Jesus did not come to give us another free meal. Jesus came to give us salvation. Here the crowd was our Lord's enemy not just because they did not have the wherewithal to help defend him. They are our Lord's enemy because they detracted from his message. Throughout the gospels, we hear Jesus telling those who had followed him not to tell of what he has done for them. For millennia, people have tried to figure out why. From the perspective of the crowd, it seems pretty clear.

Jesus does not want to be known as someone who hands out free lunches, who is a healer, and he certainly does not want to be known as someone who wants us to be rich. The crowd was Jesus' enemy because they clouded his identity. He was, and is, above all, Savior.

Voyeurism

A Reading
Matthew 21:7-9

A Meditation
We get this creepy word from the Latin *videre* and then the French *voi* both meaning "to see." During the mid-nineties, Americans got a first-hand glimpse of what it was to be a voyeur, if only through television. People have been trying to figure out why thousands of people lined up beside the Los Angeles freeway to watch OJ Simpson lead the cops on a very slow chase in his white bronco. And those of us who were watching at home have been trying to figure out why we couldn't just turn the television off. For myself, I know I had little interest in what happened to this minor celebrity. I grieved for the lives that had been lost, but still I could not turn the set off. And it continued into the summer and into the fall of that year as the OJ trial made daily news, often interrupting "regularly scheduled programming." The trial was such a circus that by the time America had lived through the horror of Oklahoma City, also in the mid-nineties, they were desperate to see our court system act with concern for justice. Such a desirable outcome was impossible because of the circus surrounding the OJ trial.

The horror of the F.W. Murrah explosion sobered America almost instantly. All too often Christians are waiting for God to do something exciting, something worth watching in their midst. Eternal salvation is not enough. It is not enough for many people I think, for two reasons.

First of all, they don't think they're that bad. I believe that is the main reason the OJ trial was of such interest. At least I never killed anybody, I can just hear many in America saying.

Secondly, their relationship with God is entirely self-serving, just like much of America's relationship with OJ and the whole trial experience. Such a crowd surrounded Jesus as he entered Jerusalem that day. They took part in his brutal death by making use of his arrival to entertain themselves and make themselves feel important, in much the same way that America made use of the OJ trial.

God forgive us for waiting until 168 people were killed in Oklahoma City to remember that justice cannot be served when a community or a nation is selfish and self-serving. Nor can we hope to remember heaven unless our relationship with God fills us with love and the desire to serve, not the desire to be entertained or to make us feel important. You would think that knowing that God of the universe died for you would be enough.

Pastor: Let us pray:
Congregation: Holy Lamb of God, protect us from ourselves, from our false desires and shallow intentions and point us to you so that we may point your love out to the world and lift it up and away from the death it seems bent on. Fill us with the life you died to give us, bring us into eternal life right now so we may proclaim that life to the world. In your sweet name we pray. Amen.

Primitive Hymn by Charles Wesley sung to "Martyrdom" the tune of "Alas and Did My Savior Bleed"

> O that I could my Lord receive,
> Who did the world redeem,

Who gave his life that I might live
A life concealed in him!

Mercy I ask to seal my peace,
That, kept by mercy's power,
I may from every evil cease,
And never grieve thee more

Now if thy gracious will it be,
E'en now, my sins remove,
And set my soul at liberty
By thy victorious love.

In answer to ten thousand prayers,
Thou pardoning God, descend;
Number me with salvation's heirs,
My sins and troubles end.

Nothing I ask or want beside,
Of all in earth or heaven,
But let me feel thy blood applied,
And live and die forgiven.

Manipulate

A Reading
Matthew 27:15-26

A Meditation
So far today as we consider our Lord's sacrifice for us and as we consider the last and perhaps most guilty party responsible for our Lord's death, we have seen the crowd betray our Savior with its desperation, its greed, and its self-centered curiosity. Now we come to its last act against Jesus. Manipulated by the chief priests and the elders, the crowd finally and completely turn on Jesus. The word manipulate

means literally to lead by the hand. But that does not mean we are members of that crowd, for that is exactly what we are, members of the crowd that daily, if not hourly, betray our Savior with our lack of trust and unwillingness to care for the world God gave us, simply because we have been manipulated by the world and the powers in it, does not mean that we are not to blame. We are surely to blame.

Discovering that Jesus will not solve our problems this side of heaven will not lift us out of our physical, emotional, and financial difficulty, we betray him by finding a way around them that involves some sort of betrayal of God's love. Discovering that in obeying Jesus, we will not be immediately showered with the gifts of this world, we either desert him or re-imagine him as a god who wants us to be rich. Discovering that the rest of the world no longer thinks believing in God is the shoe-in to the upper echelons of society that it once was, that watching Jesus will end eventually with us watching an ultimate loser, we desert him and take the lesser good with the quicker reward, seemingly sweeter but hollow and destined to disappear.

We are no different than the crowd that screamed for Jesus' blood. We allow the powers that seem to be in control to manipulate us because the rewards are obvious but short-lived, and the eternal rewards Jesus promises seem to us to be too far off. We are the crowd that betrayed our Lord. More so than Judas, the high priest, Peter, Herod, or Pilate, we the crowd, those he came to save, we betrayed our Savior to his death.

The Offering

The Prayers of the People

Closing Hymn
"Were You There?"

The congregation will leave in silence.

EASTER SUNRISE SERVICE
A Witness to the Resurrection

Opening Hymn
"Jesus Christ Is Ris'n Today"

Opening Prayer
Pastor: Let us pray:
Congregation: You have resurrected us, Christ Jesus. You have made us new. In your death, you buried our sin. In your rising you have shown us heaven. Raise our lives into your kingdom, now, so that we may resurrect the world. We pray in your name. Amen.

First Lesson
Acts 10:34-43

Easter Confession
Whenever an angel delivering messages from your own heart visited one of your servants, the first words out of that heavenly mouth were always, "Do not be afraid." It seems that we are even afraid of your messengers. We are afraid of everything.
Even you, Lord, especially you. All that you have given us, all that you have done for us, how you obviously love us, none of these things quell our fear or embolden our spirits.
How then are we to struggle against things that draw us away from you, things that we may well find less fearsome? Compared to facing the one who made the oceans and carved the canyons, confrontation and alienation may seem easy to handle. Are we to admit that you, being so far beyond our understanding, are the most fearsome thing we face?
If that is the case, should we not have reason to live in fear? Such would indeed be true if we did not have the

assurance of your powerful and never-ending love. It is true that you created the atom and fashioned day and night. You also came for us. You sent your Son for us.

You sent your Son as a stranger to live the servant's life and in so doing, you have placed us not only in the role of the stranger so that we live knowing our true home is in heaven, you have also blessed us with the servant's life.

We face the things we fear knowing that we belong completely to you and that our peace is found in your arms and nowhere else. Such a servant's life enables us to endure even the hardest things. Illness, loneliness, and poverty are things we may offer up to you. Truly, we have not one thing to fear. Truly, you have come for us. Truly, you are with us. Truly, you will bring us to yourself.

Second Lesson
Colossians 3:1-4

Hymn
"Now All the Vault of Heav'n Resound"

Gospel Lesson
Matthew 28:1-10

The Sermon

The Prayers of the People

Pastor: O Lord Jesus Christ, who upon this day did conquer death and rise from the dead, and who are alive for ever more, help us never to forget your risen presence forever with us. Lord in your mercy,
Congregation: Hear our prayer.
Pastor: Help us to remember that you are with us in every time of perplexity to guide and to direct; Lord in your mercy,

Congregation: Hear our prayer.
Pastor: That you are with us in every time of sorrow to comfort and console; Lord in your mercy,
Congregation: Hear our prayer.
Pastor: That you are with us in every time of temptation to strengthen and to inspire; Lord in your mercy,
Congregation: Hear our prayer.
Pastor: That you are with us in every time of loneliness to cheer and befriend; Lord in your mercy,
Congregation: Hear our prayer.
Pastor: That you are with us even in death to bring us to the glory of your side. Lord in your mercy,
Congregation: Hear our prayer.
Pastor: Make us to be certain that there is nothing in time or in eternity that can separate us from you, so that in your presence we may meet life with gallantry and death without fear. Lord in your mercy,
Congregation: Hear our prayer.
Pastor: You turn our darkness into light, in your light we shall see light.
Congregation: In your redeeming name, we pray. Amen.

The Offering

Holy Communion
Pastor: The Lord is with you.
Congregation: And also with you.
Pastor: Lord, you are the God of love and life. Forgive us when we give into fear. Help us, Lord, to trust in you as the maker of life and death. Help us in all things to show your Son's patient love.
Congregation: Amen. Come, Lord Jesus.
Pastor: Let us encourage each other with our Lord's command to us.

Congregation: In the night in which he was betrayed, our Lord Jesus took bread and gave thanks, broke it, and gave it to his disciples saying, "Take and eat; this is my body, given for you. Do this for the remembrance of me." Again, after supper, he took the cup, gave thanks, and gave it for all to drink saying, "This cup is the new covenant in my blood, shed for you and for all people for the forgiveness of sin. Do this for the remembrance of me."
Pastor: Lord, remember us in your kingdom and teach us to pray:
Congregation: Our Father in heaven, hallowed be your name, your kingdom come, your will be done, on earth as in heaven. Give us today our daily bread; and forgive us our sins as we forgive those who sin against us. Save us from the time of trial and deliver us from evil. For the kingdom, the power, and the glory are yours, now and forever. Amen.

The Distribution
Pastor: May the body and blood of our Lord and Savior Jesus Christ strengthen you and keep you in his grace.
Congregation: Amen.

The Closing Hymn
"I Know the Redeemer Lives"

The Word Has Come Down
Easter Sunrise Sermon

A Witness to the Resurrection
She doesn't know, but I have been awake for hours waiting for her knock on my door. It comes, and I get up and tell her I will join her in a minute. I just pray that this is where it ends. And just think, a week ago, I prayed that it would never

end. A week ago, I thought I was beginning to understand. I thought that we were going to be able to make some changes. I thought, well, I guess it really doesn't matter what I thought. Enough of this feeling sorry for myself. She's out there waiting, and I can tell from her voice that she is feeling the same way I am. Although, I'm not sure how I am feeling. Angry? Angry at whom? At the Sanhedrin for not giving him a chance? At the Romans for being here? At him for dying? All of the above I'm afraid. Afraid, yes, I never hoped to see the things I have seen in the last three days. Sad? I am drowning in it. Off we go. I see she is in high gear. I guess that is one way of handling it. Me. It's all I can do to put one foot in front of another. I keep wondering where it all went wrong. The morning air is cold. I'm shaking with it. That might be lack of sleep, too. It is true I have been up for hours. Like about 72 of them. It seems like I have no control over where my mind is going. Unbidden into my brain keep coming these things that seem not to make any sense, but at the same time beg to be remembered and pursued to their conclusion, however illogical and confusing that conclusion may be.

I should have known from the very beginning that this movement could not survive. The first time I heard him, he told a huge group of us that if we are slapped on one side of the face, we should turn our cheeks and allow the other side of our faces to be slapped. I cannot think about that now. It just reminds me of Thursday night. What they did to him before they killed him. They all seemed so angry. Some of them even seemed scared of him. I guess I can kind of understand that reaction. I would have willingly died for him and still, even now that he is dead, I am a little afraid of him. He was always saying frightening, strange, and wonderful things. I don't know how many times he said that he was going to suffer much and give up his life for the good of many. I never really knew what he meant — especially since he also said that he would rise from the dead. That kind of talk is not helpful. I'm sorry Jesus, but it just isn't. It makes no sense and it just scares people. But then I think about all the people who came to him with the most terrible problems and how he helped them all. Like that woman who had been bleeding for twelve years. I stood there and heard her voice instantly strengthen and watched her shoulders relax and color come back to her face. That happened on the same day he brought that little girl back to life.

Oh, I'm lagging behind again. If I am not careful, she will become vexed with me. Now that is a thought that has not occurred to me in years. In three years, to be exact. Not only did Jesus help us to see the world in a new way. He helped us to see ourselves and each other in a new way. He taught us how much God loved us all, especially those of us who had not been shown very much love in our lives. He reminded us that the law tells us to love our neighbors as we love ourselves. Right now that is a hard thing for me to do, to love some of my neighbors after what I have seen some of them do this past week. But with all he went through, with the anguish I know he must have felt when he screamed to God from the cross, still he never seemed to be afraid, as if he knew that no matter what happened, God would always be with him and that he would always be with God. Maybe that is what he meant when he said, after he had shared his last meal with the twelve, that he would share wine again with his Father in heaven. Maybe if he shares it with God, then maybe.

What is with her anyway? She almost seems excited. She told me that she wanted to know that she could do this small thing for him. But there is something else. Could she be thinking what I am beginning to think? Could she be thinking that his promise to conquer death means that death no longer will hold us, that maybe, we too could be with God eternally, be with him eternally. Is that what she is thinking?

I hope not. One of us has to remain sane. Speaking of which, I just remembered something. There is that big stone in the way. Who is going to move it? After all, we are just women. I know that that means the authorities won't roust us for being close to his tomb, but it also means that no one is going to be there to move the stone.

Wait a minute. Where's the stone? What is going on? Oh, no. What else have they done? What is he saying? Why seek ye the living among the dead. Jesus is dead, isn't he? After all, you and I, we know. We were there. Yes. He did tell us that he would rise from the dead. We have to go. We have to tell!